In the Name of Allah, The All-Merciful,
The Kindest towards believers.

Disclaimer

All rights reserved. No part of this publication may be reproduced, stored in a retrieval system, or transmitted in any form or by any means, electronic, mechanical, photocopying, recording, or otherwise, without the prior written permission of the publisher, except in the case of brief quotations quoted in articles or reviews.

Contact: admin@islamiclessonsmadeeasy.com.au

Visit us:
Facebook.com/islamiclessonsmadeeasy
Youtube.com/islamiclessonsmadeeasy
Instagram.com/islamic_lessons_me
Islamiclessonsmadeeasy.com.au
Ilme.net.au

The pictures used are the property of Islamic Lessons Made Easy. The content and rulings are taken from various leading scholars and are presented in a simplified manner. Therefore, for the exact definition and explanation, please refer to the original sources.

First Edition
©Copyright 2025 Islamic Lessons Made Easy

Contents

Transliteration — 4

Introduction — 5

Etiquettes of Qurān — 6

Sūrah al-Ikhlāṣ — 8

Summary — 22

Glossary — 30

Transliteration

ا	a	ق	q
ب	b	ك	k
ت	t	ل	l
ث	th	م	m
ج	j	ن	n
ح	ḥ	ه	h
خ	kh	و	w
د	d	ي	y
ذ	dh	ئ / آ / ـا	ā
ر	r	ـِي	ī
ز	z	ـُو	ū
س	s		
ش	sh		
ص	ṣ		
ض	ḍ		
ط	ṭ		
ظ	ẓ		
ع	ʿ		
غ	gh		
ف	f		

ء	Read with a sudden pause of air.
ﷺ	Blessings of Allah be upon him and his family.
عليها السلام	Peace be upon her.
عليه السلام	Peace be upon him.
سبحانه وتعالى	Glorious and Exalted Is He.

Introduction

Tafsīr is an Arabic word that means 'explanation'; it helps us understand what the verses of the Qurān really mean. Scholars study the Qurān by looking at its language, the history behind the verses and other aspects. They also think about how the verses were revealed and how we can use these teachings in our daily lives.

Tafsīr helps us connect with our faith and learn how to use the lessons of the Qurān today. It makes the wisdom of the Qurān easier to understand and more useful for us.

When we made this *Tafsīr*, we worked hard to gather ideas from trusted scholars and important books. We wanted to explain the Qurān in a way that is easy for you to understand.

We hope this *Tafsīr* helps you on your journey to learn more about the Qurān and your faith.

Etiquettes of Qurān

Before reciting, it is recommended to say:

أَعُوذُ بِاللَّهِ مِنَ الشَّيْطَانِ الرَّجِيمِ

Aʿūdhu billāhi minash shayṭānir rajīm

I seek refuge with Allah from the accursed devil.

Then say:

بِسْمِ اللَّهِ الرَّحْمَٰنِ الرَّحِيمِ

Bismillāhir Raḥmānir Raḥīm

In the name of Allah, The Most Gracious, The Most Merciful.

- Make sure you have performed *Wuḍū* before touching any verse of the Qurān
- When reading the Qurān, it is better to face the *Qiblah*
- Make sure that the place where the Qurān is read is free from impurities
- Don't put the Qurān on the ground or anywhere it might get dirty
- Don't place anything on top of the Qurān
- When you recite the Qurān, try to pronounce the words correctly
- Take time to reflect on what the verses mean

After finishing your recitation, say:

صَدَقَ اللَّهُ الْعَلِيُّ الْعَظِيمُ

Ṣadaq Allāhul ʿAliyyul ʿAẓīm

Allah, the Sublime, the Great, has spoken the truth.

Sūrah al-Ikhlāṣ

Sūrah al-Ikhlāṣ

Sūrah al-Ikhlāṣ, also known as Sūrah al-Tawḥīd, is the 112th chapter of the Qurān. It is a short yet deeply meaningful chapter that focuses on the Oneness of Allah ﷻ.

In just a few verses, it clearly describes the unique nature of Allah ﷻ, stating that He is One, eternal and unlike anything else.

Once upon a time, there were people in Mecca who worshipped statues, believing they were the greatest gods ever.

They would often mock the Prophet ﷺ and challenge him, saying, "These are our gods. Tell us, who is this God you speak of?".

In response to their question, Sūrah al-Ikhlāṣ was revealed, providing a clear answer about the Oneness of Allah ﷻ.

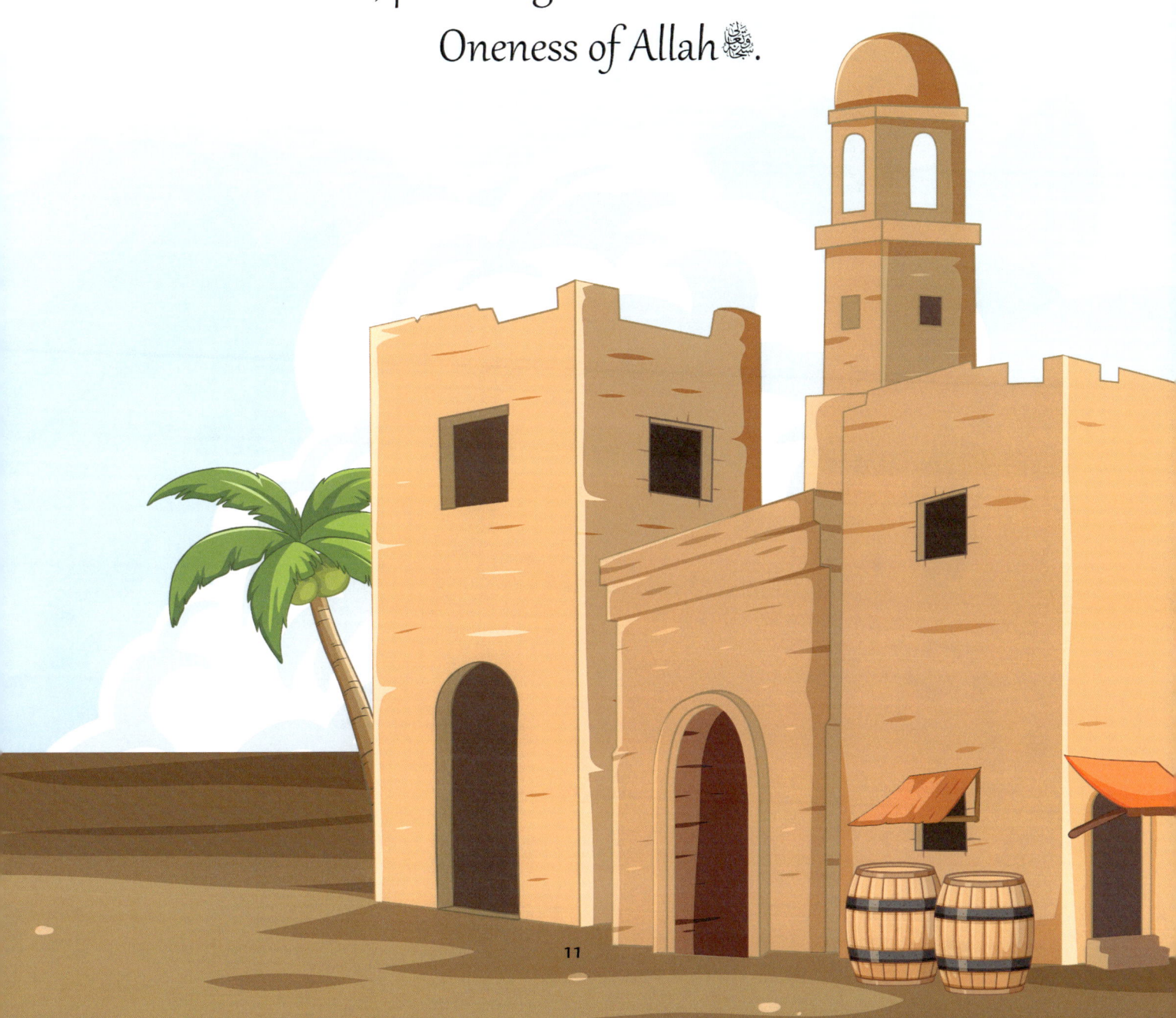

Imām al-Ṣādiq ؑ :

Whoever reads Sūrah al-Ikhlāṣ before going to sleep one hundred times, Allah ﷻ forgives fifty years of his sins.

(Al-Kāfī)

بِسْمِ اللَّهِ الرَّحْمَٰنِ الرَّحِيمِ

Bismillāhir Raḥmānir Raḥīm

In the Name of Allah, The Most Gracious,
The Most Merciful.

قُلْ هُوَ ٱللَّهُ أَحَدٌ

Qul huwallāhu aḥad

Say: He is Allah, the One, (the Unique).

The verse begins with 'Qul' (قُلْ) or 'Say' to show that the Prophet ﷺ was directly told by Allah ﷻ to deliver the message exactly as it was revealed, without changing or adding anything. This highlights how important it is to follow Allah's commands perfectly and reinforces the Prophet's role as a faithful messenger.

The word 'aḥad' (أَحَد) means One, showing that Allah ﷻ is the only God, without any equal or partners. It doesn't mean He is number one followed by other gods; it means there is no one else—just One Unique God.

ٱللَّهُ ٱلصَّمَدُ

Allāhuṣ Ṣamad

Allah is Eternal.

The word 'Ṣamad' (صَمَد) has multiple meanings.

One of its meanings is Eternal, signifying that Allah ﷻ is always alive and has no end.

Another meaning is that Allah ﷻ is completely self-sufficient, needing neither anyone nor anything to exist or thrive.

لَمْ يَلِدْ وَلَمْ يُولَدْ

Lam yalid walam yūlad

He does not give birth, nor was He born.

This means that Allah ﷻ has always existed and did not come from anything or have any children.

Unlike us, who are born from our parents and may have children of our own, Allah ﷻ is unique in every way.

وَلَمْ يَكُن لَّهُۥ كُفُوًا أَحَدٌۢ

Wa lam yakullahū kufuwan aḥad

And there is nothing like Him.

This means that Allah ﷻ is free from the qualities found in created things. For example, humans have bodies, animals need food and water, and rocks are made of minerals.

Allah ﷻ is far beyond anything you can imagine and has no equal or likeness.

Sūrah al-Ikhlāṣ, despite being short, carries a powerful message. It emphasises the absolute Oneness and uniqueness of Allah ﷻ.

Understanding this Oneness can be broken down into different levels:

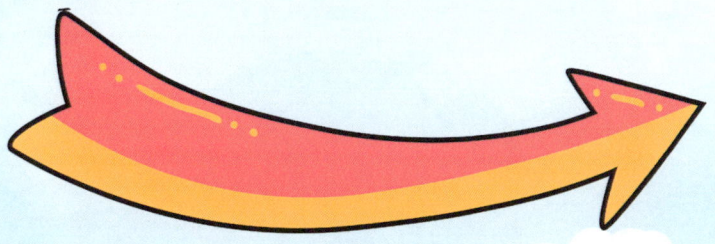

Oneness in Essence:

This means believing that there is only One God, unlike people who believe in multiple gods (like a god of rain or a god of thunder).

This *Sūrah* teaches that there is only One, incomparable God.

Oneness in Attributes:

This means the perfect attributes of Allah ﷻ, such as being All-Knowing, All-Powerful, the Creator and so on, are not separate from Him.

Unlike humans, who gain knowledge and power over time, Allah's ﷻ attributes are eternal and part of His essence.

Oneness in Actions:

This means Allah ﷻ not only created the universe but continues to sustain it. Even when we receive things from others, like money from an employer or medicine from a doctor, it is ultimately Allah ﷻ providing for us through those means.

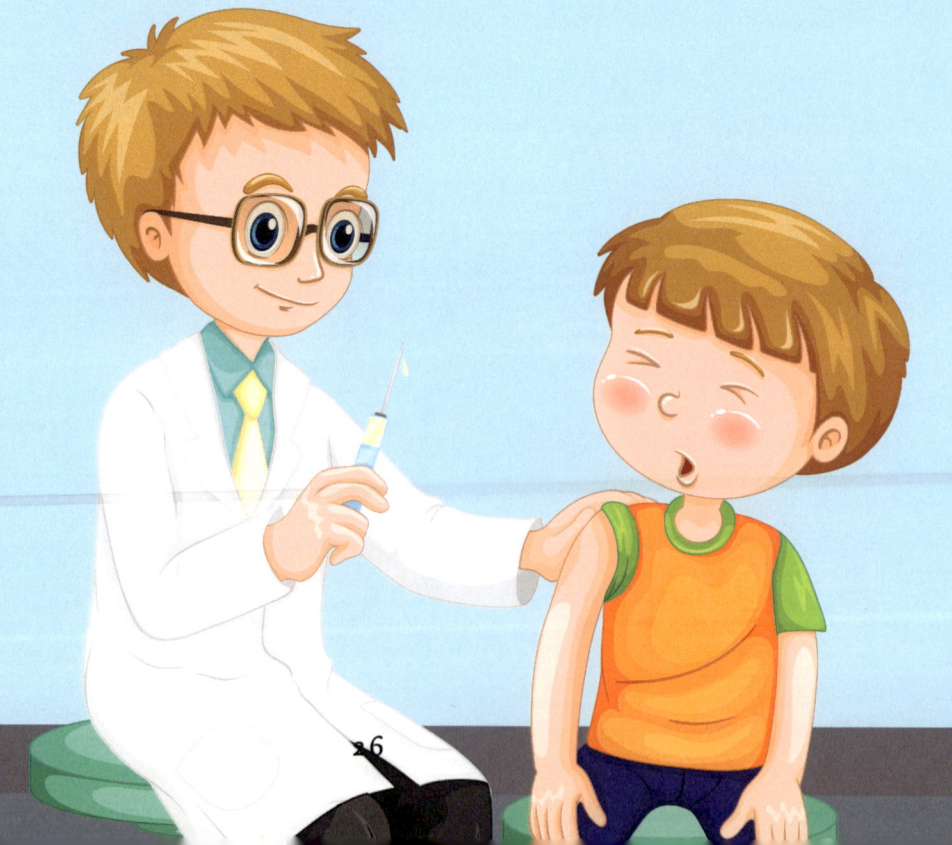

Oneness in Obedience:

This means we must obey the commands of Allah ﷻ. Whether it's respecting parents or following the guidance of the Prophet ﷺ. Disobeying Allah ﷻ shows a lack of true belief in His Oneness.

Oneness in Worship:

This means we should worship only Allah ﷻ. Sometimes people may perform acts of worship to show off, which takes the sincerity away from being purely for Allah ﷻ.

This chapter should refine and purify our belief in Allah ﷻ. The more we reflect on these ideas and bring them into our hearts, the more sincere our faith becomes.

This is why the chapter is called Sūrah al-Ikhlās, meaning 'The Sincerity'.

Glossary

Aḥad — One, Unique

Ikhlāṣ — Sincerity

Qiblah — Direction of the Kaʿbah

Qul — Say

Ṣamad — Eternal, Needless

Sūrah — Chapter

Sūrah al-Ikhlāṣ — Chapter of Sincerity

Credit

All praise belongs to Allah, the All Merciful towards all existents, the Kindest towards believers. He Who has given us enough patience and courage to complete this book.

Islamic Lessons Made Easy would like to thank all those involved in this project for their hard work and commitment.

CREATOR
Abbas Ibrahim

EDITORS
Kawthar Ibrahim
Sheikh Dr Zaid Alsalami

Allahumma ṣalli 'ala Muḥammadi(n)w wa āli Muḥammad
O Allah, (please do) bless Muḥammad and the Household of Muḥammad

Contact: Admin@islamiclessonsmadeeasy.com.au

Visit us:
Facebook.com/islamiclessonsmadeeasy
Youtube.com/islamiclessonsmadeeasy
Instagram.com/islamic_lessons_me
Islamiclessonsmadeeasy.com.au
Ilme.net.au

www.ingramcontent.com/pod-product-compliance
Lightning Source LLC
Chambersburg PA
CBRC091202070526
44583CB00008B/180